The Dubliners' Songbook

Hal Leonard
7777 West Bluemound Road,
Milwaukee, WI 53213
Email: info@halleonard.com

Hal Leonard Australia Pty. Ltd.
4 Lentara Court Cheltenham,
Victoria, 9132 Australia
Email: info@halleonard.com.au

Hal Leonard Europe Limited
42 Wigmore Street Maryleborne,
London, WIU 2 RN
Email: info@halleonardeurope.com

Most of the songs in this book are traditional. but they have been arranged and adapted by the dubliners.

Edited by Eric Winter
Designed by Graham Evernden

Cover: With acknowledgement to our friends at Arthur Guinness Son and Co. Ltd.

Contents

Introduction

Not far from St Stephen's Green, you'll find in Merrion Row, Dublin, a bar run by Paddy O'Donoghue. Ever since my first trip to Eire, I remember the bar as a mecca for folk singers and instrumentalists, so it's not surprising that the original Dubliners first met up there.

Ronnie Drew and Barney McKenna originally teamed up for a fund raising concert and went on to work in a revue with a well known comedian, John Molloy. Ronnie and Barney were, of course, frequently to be seen in O'Donoghue's, and so too were Luke Kelly and Ciaran Bourke. The first time I went into O'Donoghue's, I saw a guitar hanging on the wall behind the bar. It was Luke Kelly's - he used to leave it there between sessions.

The four lads formed a group that, for a while, was known as the Ronnie Drew group, and it was while they were travelling to a singing engagement that they decided to call themselves the Dubliners. Luke was reading James Joyce's novel of that name and put an end to all argument when he announced that, really, no other name would be better. Not for the first time he was right.

At that time (1962) I had known Luke Kelly for a couple of years. He was often seen in the London folk clubs, and even more often at Ian Campbell's Jug o' Punch club in Birmingham. My first memories of meeting the other three Dubliners arise from successive fleadanna ceoil (festivals of music, that is) in Mullingar and Clones. And the group also turned up at the Edinburgh festival in 1963.

That appearance led to the group's being featured in various editions of the BBC television show, Hootenanny. They signed with Transatlantic Records, for whom they cut a single (Rocky road to Dublin/Wild rover) and their first lp, simply titled The Dubliners.

They were doing well in Ireland, but it is no overstatement to say that they took the English folk scene by storm - clubs, concerts, and festivals. Some liked them for their rough diamond quality: although they were all manifestly good performers, they made no attempt to put a false, showbiz gloss on what they were doing, preferring to deliver it in a gutsy fashion that became almost a trademark. Some liked them for their irreverence: they didn't mind knocking anything that was going, including many of the most cherished ideas about themselves held by the Irish. Some liked them for their readiness to embrace causes they believed in: I do not ever remember commercial considerations stopping the Dubliners from making outspoken comments on national and international issues.

The Dubliners also had a reputation for being a hard-singing, hard-playing, hard-drinking lot - that last bit has been exaggerated to some extent by their admirers.

During 1964, Luke Kelly left the group for a while to pursue a solo career and Bobby Lynch took Luke's place in the line-up. By the time they made their second lp for Transatlantic, Bobby and another newcomer, John Sheehan, had both joined the Dubliners. When Luke returned, Bobby left to become a distinguished solo performer, but John stayed with the group. That line-up, Barney, Ronnie, Ciaran, Luke, and John, persists to date.

The Dubliners have gone on to become world famous. In 1967, they made a single for the now defunct Major-Minor label, Seven drunken nights, and it reached the Top Ten in Britain's hit parade. They made a number of albums for Major-Minor and are now recording for Tribune.

The Dubliners have toured in Europe, the United States, Canada, Australia, and New Zealand. It would be impossible to keep up with everything they do, but I've been lucky enough to see them in action twice over the past fourteen months - at a London concert, and in Holland at the 1971 Eindhoven festival.

It no longer surprises me to find that the group sounds as fresh as today's newspaper whenever they perform. In the autumn of 1972, they celebrated ten years of togetherness, but I've never known it to show on stage. They seem incapable of giving a stale performance.

Many of the songs the Dubliners sing are already in print, but this is the first big collection of songs chosen from their repertoire. The forty-odd songs in this book were chosen so as not to duplicate those already in print. Any selection must leave out somebody's favourite, I suppose, but I don't think you are likely to find here any songs you don't like. A few of them speak completely for themselves, but here and there I have added notes that I hope readers and singers will find informative.

Of course, many of the songs exist in 'standard' versions, and, where the texts printed here do not follow those versions it is because the Dubliners do not follow them. In places they depart from the best-known words; sometimes they add or subtract a verse; I have followed the version they actually sing on their Transatlantic and Hallmark records.

Ray Edwards (as always) helped me with the transcription of tunes that the publishers were not able to supply. Stuart Lawrence transposed and tidied the tunes, then drew the music. Mick Maloney (one-time of the Johnstons folk group) was a tower of strength when we came to the 'Dublinese' and slang words. Mary Hardy, secretary of the Dubliners' Club, filled me in on all the details of the group's history that I didn't know or couldn't accurately remember. Bob Wise of Music Sales, waited with more patience than I deserve while I solved the various problems of producing the book.

To them, and to the Dubliners who have provided me with many happy hours, my grateful thanks.

Eric Winter

London, 1974

Ciaron Bourke

   Ciaron Bourke, born in Dublin on 18 February, 1936, spent
his formative years with a Gaelic-speaking nanny and in a bi-
lingual school. He had a university education, and goodnaturedly
tolerates the cracks about it from the others, who didn't. In
the group, he plays harmonica, whistle, and guitar, and sings.

   Ciaron doesn't like town life, so he lives, with his wife
Jeannie, in a georgian house in the Dublin mountains. They
have four delightful daughters - Ciara, Laoighse, Soibhra,
and Rathfiona. He's built a magnificent fireplace from the
local granite stone.

   Long conversations in Gaelic and English are the rule
in Ciaron's completely bi-lingual household. He likes cooking,
especially of exotic spiced foods, keeps a couple of donkeys,
and has a boat in the front garden. He's waiting, he says,
for the Flood.

Barney McKenna

Barney McKenna, born in Dublin on 16 December, 1939, lives with his Dutch wife, Joka, in a seaside village overlooking Dublin bay. Since he loves sea fishing, nothing could suit him better.

Barney started playing music when he was 6, broke the strings on his uncle Jim"s mandoline and his uncle Barney"s

fiddle, and even blew his dad's melodeon out of tune. At 12, he tried to join the No 1 Irish Army band, but he was rejected for faulty vision.

At $14\frac{1}{2}$, when he left school, his banjo playing was so good that he had become an embarrassment to other musicians. Barney is an admirer of Paul Robeson, Joe Heanney, Segovia, and Julian Bream.

Barney has a marvellous ability to overcome language barriers, and his banjo has become rather like an extension of his arms. Asked to name his most memorable experience, Barney said, "Meeting my wife".

John Sheahan

John Sheahan, born in Dublin on 19 May, 1939, is a splendid instrumentalist, who excels on the fiddle. He played tin whistle whilst still at school, and went on to the Municipal School of Music to study the violin for five years, where he enlivened the classics by adding his own twiddly-bits. He won several awards at various feiseanna – festivals of Irish traditional music, dancing, poetry and literature.

John is a qualified electrician. He likes experimenting with new instruments, wiring and decorating houses, and drawing plans.

John is fond of bluegrass – irreverently dubbed cowboy music by Luke Kelly.

Sheahan's golden hair and bushy beard (the bushiest of the five, some reckon) are the outward signs of the Dubliner's quietest member, who has a delightful sense of humour. With his wife, Mary, his daughter Siobhan, and his son Fiachre, John lives in the Dublin suburb of Raheny.

Ronnie Drew

Ronnie Drew, born in Dun-Laoghaire on 16 September, 1935, was a boy soprano (would you believe?) until his voice broke. That instantly recognizable noise he makes has been described as like coke being crushed under a door.

At 19, Ronnie began to play guitar and sing during a variety of occupations in Dublin. Then he spent three years

teaching English in Spain, where he learned a lot about flamenco music.

He loves riding and owns two horses, and his pony, Bacardi, took first prize at the 1969 Dublin horse show.

With his wife Deidre, his daughter Cliona, and his son Phelim, Ronnie lives a stone's throw from St. Stephen's Green.

Luke Kelly

Luke Kelly, born in Dublin on 17 November, 1940, has a mop of red hair that looks like a sunburst. He grew up in the tough–and–tumble of Dublin's dockside, and left school at $13\frac{1}{2}$.

For a while he thought folk songs were rather square, but, when he discovered otherwise, he began to sing them. Luke is probably the most outspoken Dubliner and has always been a

rebel. His poem <u>For what died the sons of Roisin</u>? is a devastating indictment of conditions in Ireland. He plays banjo – and guitar, though not on stage.

Luke is hardly ever seen without a book or newspaper. John Sheahan says Luke would read wallpaper if there was nothing else. He likes soccer and is a keen golfer.

As an actor Luke has played in the Dublin theatre festival, and in Dublin and London productions of Brendan Behan's <u>Richard's Cork Leg</u> (with the other lads, of course).

Luke's wife Deidre O'Connell owns and runs Dublin''s Focus Theatre.

The Banks of the Roses

Traditional, arranged by the Dubliners
(c) 1963 Heathside Music Ltd.

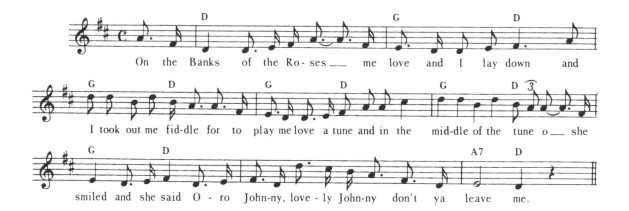

On the Banks of the Ro-ses ___ me love and I lay down and I took out me fid-dle for to play me love a tune and in the mid-dle of the tune o ___ she smiled and she said O - ro John-ny, love-ly John-ny don't ya leave me.

When I was a young man I heard me father say
That he'd rather see me dead and buried in the clay,
Sooner than be married to any runaway,
By the lovely sweet banks of the roses.

And then I am no runaway and soon I'll let them know
That I can take the bottle or can leave it alone,
And if her daddy doesn't like it he can keep his daughter at home,
And young Johnny will go rovin' with another.

And when I get married t'will be in the month of May,
When the leaves they are green and the meadows they are gay,
And me and me true love we'll sit and sport and play,
By the lovely sweet banks of the roses.

Come All Ye Tramps and Hawkers

Traditional, arranged by the Dubliners
(c) 1963 Heathside Music Ltd.

Luke collected this well known song in Scotland. It is a
truncated version of the much fuller song performed by the late
Jimmie McBeath.

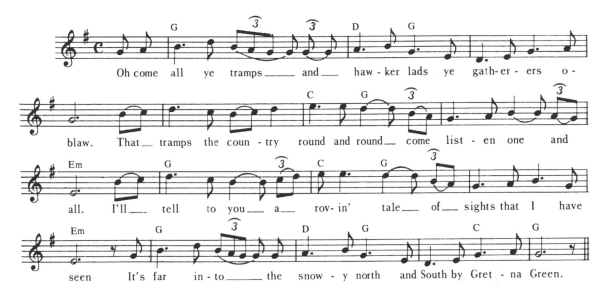

Oftimes I've laughed unto mysel' when trudgin' on the road,
My toerags round my blistered feet, my face as broon 's a toad,
Wi' lumps o' cake and tattie scones, wi' whangs o' braxie ham,
Nae gi'en a thocht tae whaur I've been an' less tae whaur I'm gan.

I've done my share o' humpin' wi' the dockers on the Clyde,
I've helpit Buckie trawlers haul their herrin's o'er the side,
I've helped tae build yon michty bridge that spans the busy Forth,
Wi' mony an Angus farmer, I've ploo'ed the bonnie earth.

I'm happy in the summer time beneath the bricht blue sky,
No thinkin' in the mornin' whaur at nicht I'm ga'en tae lie
In barn or byre or anywhere, dossin' oot among the hay,
An' if the weather treats me right I'm happy every day.

Boolavogue

Traditional, arranged by the Dubliners
(c) 1963 Heathside Music Ltd.

The song appears in various forms under this title or as <u>Father Murphy</u> —
he was one of the 'croppy priests' in the rising of 1798 at Wexford.

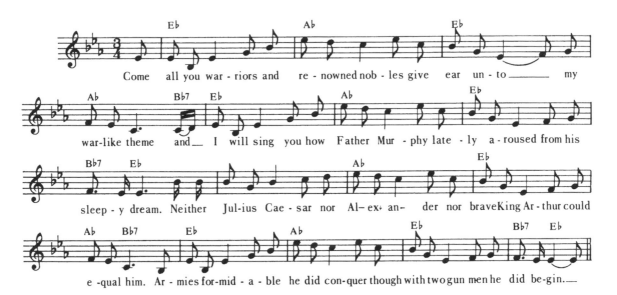

Come all you warriors and renowned nobles give ear unto my war-like theme and I will sing you how Father Murphy lately aroused from his sleepy dream. Neither Julius Caesar nor Alexander nor brave King Arthur could equal him. Armies formidable he did conquer though with two gunmen he did begin.

Camolin cavalry he did unhorse them,
Their first lieutenant he cut them down,
With shattered ranks, and with broken columns,
They soon returned to Camolin town.
On the hill of Oulart he displayed his valour,
Where a hundred Corkmen lay on the plain
At Enniscorthy his sword he wielded
And I hope to see him once more again

When Enniscorthy became subject to him,
Twas then to Wexford we marched our men
And on the Three Rock took up our quarters,
Waiting for daylight the town to win.
The loyal townsmen gave their assistance
We'll die or conquer, they all did say,
The yeomen cavalry made no resistance,
For on the pavement their corpses lay

With drums a-beating the town did echo,
And acclamations came from door to door.
On the Windmill Hill we pitched our tents,
And we drank like heroes, but paid no score.
On Carraig Rua for some time we waited,
And next to Gorey we did repair,
At Tubberneering we thought no harm,
The bloody army was waiting there

The issue of it was a close engagement,
While on the soldiers we played warlike pranks;
Thro' sheepwalks, hedgerows and shady thickets,
There were mangled bodies and broken ranks.
The shuddering cavalry I can't forget them;
We raised the brushes on their helmets straight,
They turned about, and they bid for Dublin,
As if they ran for a ten-pound plate.

Some crossed Donnybrook and more through Blackrock,
And some up Shankill without wound or flaw,
And, if Barry Lawless be not a liar,
There's more went groaning up Luggelaw.
To the Windmill Hill of Enniscorthy
The British Fencibles they fled like deers,
But our ranks were tattered, and sorely scattered,
By the loss of Kyan and the Shelmaleers.

The streets of England were left quite naked
Of all its army, both foot and horse.
The highlands of Scotland were left unguarded,
Likewise the Hessians the seas they crossed.
But, if the Frenchmen had reinforced us
And landed transports in Bagenbun,
Father John Murphy would be their seconder
And sixteen thousand with him would come.

Success attend the sweet County Wexford
Throw off its yoke and to battle run.
Let them not think we gave up our arms,
For every man has a pike and gun.

The Dublin Fusiliers

Well you've heard about the wars between the Russians and the Brits,
The sar' one day was reading an ould copy of 'Titbits'
And when the General came to him and threw himself down in tears,
'We'd better run back like blazes, here's the Dublin Fusiliers.'
The sar' commenced to tremble and he bit his underlip.
'Begorra boys!' says he, 'I think we'd better take the tip
The devil's come from Dublin and to judge from what I hears
They're demons of militia men, the Dublin Fusiliers.'

Well the serjeant cried, 'Get ready lads, lay down each sword and gun,
Take off your shoes and stockings boys, and when I tell yous, run.
They didn't stop but started and amidst three ringing cheers,
Came a shower of bricks and bullets from the Dublin Fusiliers.
The time that Julius Caesar tried to land down at Ringsend,
The coastguards couldn't stop them, so for the Dublins they did send,
And, just as they were landing, lads, we heard three ringing cheers:
'Get back to Rome like blazes here's the Dublin Fusiliers.'

Easy and Slow

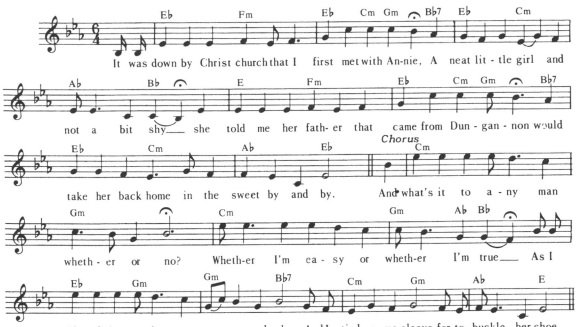

It was down by Christ church that I first met with An-nie, A neat lit-tle girl and not a bit shy___ she told me her fath-er that came from Dun-gan-non would take her back home in the sweet by and by.

Chorus
And what's it to a-ny man wheth-er or no? Wheth-er I'm ea-sy or wheth-er I'm true___ As I lift-ed her pet-ti-coat ea-sy and slow, And I tied up me sleeve for to buckle her shoe.

All along Thomas Street down to the Liffey,
The sunshine was gone and the evening grew dark.
Along by King's Bridge and begod in a jiffey
Me arms were around her beyant in the park.

From city or country a girl's a jewel,
And well known for gripping the most of them are.
But any young fella is really a fool
If he tries at the first time for to go a bit far.

And if ever you go to the town of Dungannon
You can search till your eyeballs are empty or blind,
Be yeh lyin' or walkin' or sittin' or runnin',
A girl like Annie you never will find

Fa-La-La-La-Lo-Horo

Traditional, arranged by the Dubliners
(c) 1964 Heathside Music Ltd.

A Scottish song learned from the singing of Ray and Archie Fisher.

Hey fa la la lo, ho ro air fa la la lay,____ Hey fa la la
lo ho ro, air fa la la lay____ Hey fa la la lo ho ro air
fa la la lay,____ Fal dee fal o ho ro, air fa la la lay.____

The song that I sing's a song of laughter and love.
There's a tang o' the sea and blue from heaven above,
Of reason there's none and why should there be forby?
With fire in my blood and toe, and a light in the eye.

The heather's ablaze with bloom and the myrtle is sweet,
There's a song in the air, the road's a song at our feet,
So step it along as light as a bird on the wing,
And while we are stepping we join our voices and sing.

And whether the blood be highland, lowland or no
And whether the skin be white or black as a sloe,
Of kith and of kin where one be as right be as wrong,
As long as our hearts be true to the lilt of a song.

The Foggy Dew

Traditional, arranged by the Dubliners
(c) 1966 Heathside Music Ltd.

Not to be confused with the English song of the same name, this
moving ballad concerns the Easter rising of 1916.

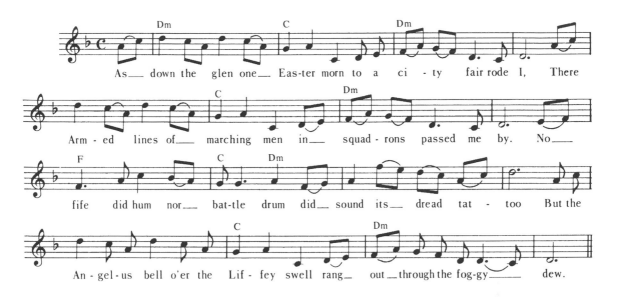

As— down the glen one— Eas-ter morn to a ci - ty fair rode I, There
Arm - ed lines of— marching men in— squad - rons passed me by. No—
fife did hum nor— bat-tle drum did— sound its— dread tat - too But the
An - gel-us bell o'er the Lif - fey swell rang— out — through the fog-gy— dew.

Right proudly high over Dublin Town they hung out the flag of war
'Twas better to die 'neath an Irish sky than at Sulva or Sud El Bar;
And from the plains of Royal Meath strong men came hurrying through,
While Britannia's Huns, with their long range guns, sailed in through
the Foggy Dew.

'Twas Britannia bade our Wild Geese go that small nations might be free,
But their lonely graves are by Sulva's waves or the shore of
the Great North Sea.
O, had they died by Pearse's side, or had fought with Cathal Brugha,
Their names we would keep where the fenians sleep, 'neath the shroud
of the Foggy Dew.

But the bravest fell, and the requiem bell rang mournfully and clear
For those who died that Eastertide in the springtime of the year.
And the world did gaze, in deep amaze, at those fearless men, but few,
Who bore the fight that freedom's light might shine through
the Foggy Dew.

Finnegan's Wake

Traditional, arranged by the Dubliners
(c) 1966 Heathside Music Ltd.

Dedicated, no doubt, to the Irishman's love of funerals and
Whiskey, this song is extremely well known on the British club
scene. It supplied the leitmotif for James Joyce's famous novel.

One morning Tim was rather full,
His head felt heavy which made him shake,
He fell off the ladder and he broke his skull,
And they carried him home his corpse to wake,
Well they rolled him up in a nice clean sheet,
And they laid him out upon the bed,
With a bottle of whiskey at his feet,
And a barrel of porter at his head.

Well his friends assembled at the wake,
And Mrs. Finnegan called for lunch,
Well first they brought in tay and cake,
Then pipes, tobacco, and brandy punch.
Then Widow Malone began to cry,
'Such a lovely corpse, did you ever see,
Arrah, Tim avourneen, why did you die?'
'Will ye hould your gob?' said Molly McGee.

Well Mary O'Connor took up the job,
'Biddy,' says she, 'you're wrong, I'm sure,'
Well Biddy gave her a belt in the gob,
And left her sprawling on the floor;
Well civil war did then engage,
Woman to woman and man to man,
Shillelagh law was all the rage,
And a row and a ruction soon began.

Well Tim Maloney raised his head,
When a bottle of whiskey flew at him,
He ducked and, landing on the bed,
The whiskey scattered over Tim;
Bedad he revives, see how he rises,
Tim Finnegan rising in the bed,
Saying, 'Whittle your whiskey around like blazes,
T'underin' Jaysus, do ye think I'm dead?'

The Glendalough Saint

Traditional, arranged by the Dubliners
(c) 1966 Heathside Music Ltd.

A thoroughly disrespectful song about St Kevin, but, as James N.
Healy says in The Second Book of Irish Ballads, 'the disrespect
smells more of affection **than** impiety'.

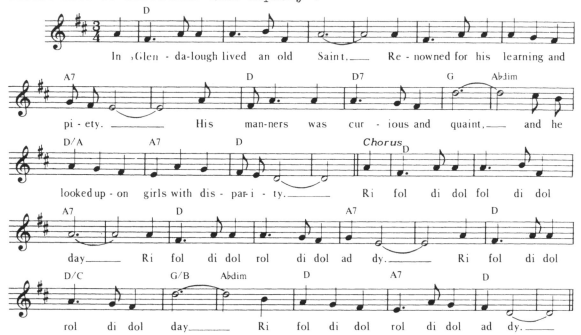

He was fond of readin' a book
When he could get one to his wishes.
He was fond of castin' his hook
In among the ould fishes.

But one evenin' he landed a trout,
He landed a fine big trout, sir,
When young Kathleen from over the way
Came to see what the ould monk was about, sir.

'Oh get out o' me way,' said the saint,
'For I am a man of great piety,
And me good manners I wouldn't taint
By mixing with female society.'

Oh but Kitty she wouldn't give in
And when he got home to his rockery,
He found she was seated therein,
A-polishin' up his ould crockery.

Well he gave the poor creature a shake
And I wish that the Garda had got him!
For he threw her right into the lake,
And, be Jaysus, she sank to the bottom.

The Greenland Whale Fisheries

Traditional, arranged by the Dubliners
(c) 1964 Heathside Music Ltd.

The lookout on the mainmast he stood
His spyglass in his hand
'There's a whale, there's a whale, there's a whalefish,' he cried,
'And he blows at every span, brave boys,
And he blows at every span.'

The captain stood on the quarter deck,
The ice was in his eye.
'Overhaul, overhaul, let your jib sheets fall
And go put your boats to sea, brave boys,
And go put your boats to sea.'

The boats were lowered and the men put out,
The whale was full in view
Resolved, resolved was each whalerman bold
For to steer where the whalefish blew, brave boys,
For to steer where the whalefish blew.

The harpoon struck and the line paid out.
With a single flourish of his tail,
He capsized our boat and we lost five men
And we did not catch that whale, brave boys,
And we did not catch that whale.

The losin' of them five jolly men,
It grieved our captain sore,
But the losin' of that sperm whale fish,
Oh it grieved him ten times more, brave boys,
Oh it grieved him ten times more.

'Up anchor now,' our captain he cried,
'For the winter stars do appear,
And it's time we left this cold country,
And for the homeland we did steer, brave boys,
And for the homeland we did steer.

Well Greenland is a barren land,
A land that bears no green,
Where there's ice and snow, and the whalefishes blow,
And the daylight's seldom seen, brave boys,
And the daylight's seldom seen.

The Holy Ground

Traditional, arranged by the Dubliners
(c) 1963 Heathside Music Ltd.

The Dubliners wouldn't dispute that this song was made very
popular by the Clancy Brothers and Tommy Makem. The Holy Ground
was a renowned place for prostitution, in Cobh, co Cork.

See the storm a-rising,
I see it coming soon,
And the sky it is so cloudy
You can scarcely see the moon.
And the good old ship, she was tossing about,
The riggin' was all tore,
And still I live with hopes to see,
The Holy Ground once more.
    Fine girl you are!

And now the storm is over
And we are safe on shore,
We will drink a toast to the Holy Ground
And the girls that we adore.
We will drink strong ale and porter
And make the rafters roar,
And when our money is all spent,
We'll go to sea for more.
    Fine girl you are!

Home Boys Home

Traditional, arranged by the Dubliners
(c) 1963 Heathside Music Ltd.

Oh well, who wouldn't be a sailor lad a sailin' on the main, To gain the good will of his captain's good name? He came ashore one evening for to be, And that was the beginning of my own true love and me. And it's home, boys home, home, I'd like to be home for a while In me own country, where the oak and the ash and the bonny rowan tree are all a-growin' green in the old country.

Well I asked her for a candle for to light me up to bed
And likewise for a handkerchief to tie around me head.
She tended to me needs like a young maid ought to do,
So then I says to her, 'Now won't you leap in with me too?'

Well she jumped into bed, making no alarm,
Thinking a young sailor lad could do to her no harm.
Well I hugged her and I kissed her the whole night long,
Till she wished the short night had been nine years long.

Well early next morning the sailor lad arose
And into Mary's apron threw a handful of gold
Saying, 'Take this me dear for the mischief that I've done
For tonight I fear I've left you with a daughter or a son'.

'Well, if it be a girl child, send her out to nurse,
With gold in her pocket and with silver in her purse,
And if it be a boy child he'll wear the jacket blue
And go climbing up the rigging like his daddy used to do.'

Oh come all of you fair maidens, a warning take by me,
And never let a sailor lad an inch above your knee,
For I trusted one and he beguiled me,
He left me with a pair of twins to dangle on me knee.

Hot Asphalt

Traditional, arranged by the Dubliners
(c) 1966 Heathside Music Ltd.

Some regard this song as stage Irish, but that doesn't seem to
have affected its popularity. It has attracted several parodies.

The other night a copper comes and he says to me, 'McGuire
Would you kindly let me light me pipe down at your boiler fire?'
And he planks himself right down in front, with hobnails up, till late,
And says I, 'Me dacent man, you'd better go and find your bate'
He ups and yells, 'I'm down on you, I'm up to all yer pranks,
Don't I know you for a traitor from the Tipperary ranks?'
Boys, I hit straight from the shoulder and I gave him such a belt
That I knocked him into the boiler full of hot asphalt.

We quickly dragged him out again and we threw him in the tub,
And with soap and warm water we began to rub and scrub,
But devil the thing, it hardened and it turned him hard as stone
And with every other rub sure you could hear the copper groan.
'I'm thinkin', says O'Reilly, 'that he's lookin' like Ould Nick,
And burn me if I'm not inclined to claim him with me pick.'
'Now,' says I, 'it would be 'asier to boil him till he melts,
And to stir him nice and 'asy in the hot asphalt.

You may talk about yer sailorlads, ballad singers and the rest,
Your shoemakers and your tailors but we please the ladies best.
The only ones who know the way their flinty hearts to melt
Are the lads around the boiler making hot asphalt.
With rubbing and with scrubbing sure I caught me death of cold,
And for scientific purposes me body it was sold,
In the Kelvingrove museum me boys, I'm hangin' in me pelt,
As a monument to the Irish mixing hot asphalt.

I'll Tell Me Ma

Traditional, arranged by the Dubliners
(c) 1963 Heathside Music Ltd.

Wherever schoolkids gather, there seems to be a version of I'll
Tell Me Ma. The city varies accordingly — Dublin, Belfast, Glasgow, etc.

Albert Mooney says he loves her,
All the boys are fightin' for her,
Knock at the door and ring at the bell
And 'Oh, me true love, are you well?'
Out she comes, white as snow,
Rings on her fingers, bells on her toes
Ould Johnny Morrissey says she'll die,
If she doesn't get the fella with the roving eye.

Let the wind and the rain and the hail blow high
And the snow come travellin' through the sky,
She's as nice as apple pie,
She'll get her own lad by and by.
When she gets a lad of her own,
She won't tell her ma when she gets home.
Let them all come as they will,
It's Albert Mooney she loves still.

A Jar of Porter

Traditional, arranged by the Dubliners
(c) 1963 Heathside Music Ltd.

Too - ra loo - ra   loo ra la,   too ra loo ra   loo ra la,   too   ra loo ra

loo ra   la give the child a   jar of   por - ter   If   you want your child to grow,— your

child to grow, your child to grow,   If you want your child to grow give him   a jar of   por-ter.(sing)

When I was young and cradle cake,
No drop of milk now would I take.
Me father up and had his spake
    'Give the child a drop of porter'.

When I am dead and in my grave,
I hope for me a prayer you'll say,
And if you're passing by that you'll
    Throw in a jar of porter.

And when I reach the golden gates,
I hope I'll not have long to wait,
I'll call Saint Peter aside and say
    'Brought you a jar of porter.'

Johnson's Motor Car

Traditional, arranged by the Dubliners
(c) 1963 Heathside Music Ltd.

A fairly modern song that speaks for itself. It has passed
successfully into the tradition.

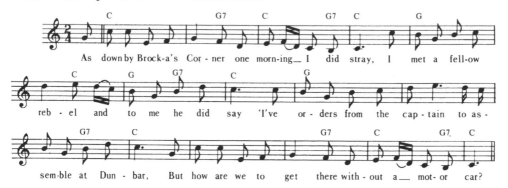

As down by Brock-a's Cor-ner one morn-ing— I did stray, I met a fell-ow
reb-el and to me he did say 'I've or-ders from the cap-tain to as-
sem-ble at Dun-bar, But how are we to get there with-out a— mot-or car?

Oh, Barney dear, be of good cheer and I'll tell you what we'll do.
The Specials they are plentiful and the IRA are few.
We'll wire up to Stranorlar before we walk that far
And we'll give the boys a jolly good ride in Johnson's motor car.

When Dr Johnson got that wire he soon put on his shoes
He said, 'This must be an urgent case and I have no time to lose.'
He put on his fancy castor hat, and on his breast a star.
You could hear the din, going through Glenfin, of Johnson's motor car.

But when he got to the railway bridge the rebels he saw there,
And Johnson knew the game was up for at him they did stare
He says, 'I have a permit for to travel near and far.'
'We don't want your English permit; we want your motor car.'

'What will my loyal brethren say when they hear the news?
My car it has been commandeered by the rebels at Dunloos,'
'We'll give you a receipt for it, all signed by Captain Barr,
And, when Ireland gets her freedom, you'll get your motor car.'

Well we set the car in motion and filled her to the brim
With guns and bayonets shining, which made old Johnson grim,
And Barney hoisted the Sinn Fein flag and it fluttered like a star
And we gave three cheers for the IRA and Johnson's motor car

Now, when the specials heard the news, they soon put on their shoes.
'They've stolen Johnson's motor car, and there is no time to lose.'
They searched around the valleys, they searched both near and far,
But the IRA were far away in Johnson's motor car.

The Leaving Of Liverpool

Traditional, arranged by the Dubliners
(c) 1964 Heathside Music Ltd.

Originally collected from Dick Maitland, ex-seaman, by W.M.
Doerflinger, who published text and tune in Shantymen And Shantyboys.
Ewan MacColl was instrumental in popularising this song on the folk scene

Fare-well to Prin-ces' land-ing stage Riv-er Mer-sey fare thee well I am
bound for Cal-i-for-ni-a A— place— I know right well. So fare thee well my
own true love when I re-turn u-ni-ted we will be. It's not the
leav-ing of Liv-er-pool that grieves me but my dar-ling when I think of thee.

I have sailed with Burgess once before,
I think I know him well.
If a man's a sailor, he will get along,
If not, then, he's sure in hell.

Farewell to Lower Frederick Street,
Anson Terrace and Park Lane,
I am bound away for to leave you,
And I'll never see you again.

I am bound for California
By way of stormy Cape Horn,
And I will write to thee a letter, love,
When I am homeward bound.

I've shipped on a Yankee clipper ship,
'Davy Crockett' is her name;
And Burgess is the captain of her,
And they say that she's a floating hell.

The Kerry Recruit

Traditional. arranged by the Dubliners
(c) 1964 Heathside Music Ltd.

A lovely, sardonic commentary popularised in the early days of
the folk revival by Seamus Ennis.

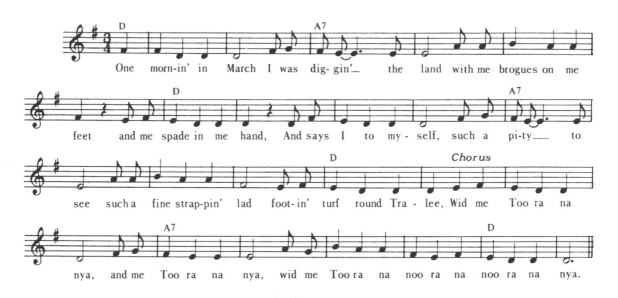

One morn-in' in March I was dig-gin'— the land with me brogues on me feet and me spade in me hand, And says I to my-self, such a pi-ty— to see such a fine strap-pin' lad foot-in' turf round Tra-lee, Wid me Too ra na nya, and me Too ra na nya, wid me Too ra na noo ra na noo ra na nya.

So I buttered me brogues, shook hands with me spade,
Then I went to the fair like a dashing young blade,
When up comes a sergeant he asks me to list
'Arra, sergeant a gra, stick the bob in me fist.'

And the first thing they gave me it was a red coat,
With a wide strap of leather to tie round me throat.
They gave me a quare thing — I asked what was that,
And they told me it was a cockade for me hat.

The next thing they gave me they called it a gun,
With powder and shot and a place for me thumb.
Well first she spat fire and then she spat smoke,
Lord, she gave a great leap and me shoulder near broke.

Well the first place they sent me was down by the quay
On board of a warship bound for the Crime'a.
Three sticks in the middle all rowled round with sheets,
Faith, she walked on the water without any feet.

When at Balaclava we landed quite soon,
Both cold wet and hungry we lay on the ground.
Next morning for action the bugle did call,
And we had a hot breakfast of powder and ball.

Well we fought at the Alma, likewise Inkermann,
And the Russians they whaled us at the Redan.
In scalin' the wall there meself lost me eye,
And a big Russian bullet ran off with me thigh.

'Twas there we lay bleeding stretched on the cold ground,
Both heads, legs and arms were all scattered around.
I thought of me mam and me cleaveens were nigh,
Sure they'd bury me decent and raise a loud cry.

Well a doctor was called and he soon staunched me blood,
And he gave me a fine elegant leg made of wood.
They gave me a medal and tenpence a day
Contented with Sheelagh, I'll live on half-pay.

The Little Beggarman

Traditional, arranged by the Dubliners
(c) 1963 Heathside Music Ltd.

Related to a much older song The Old Settoo (French: surtout =
overcoat) said to go to the tune of The White Cockade. A very
popular song in Dublin.

I am a lit-tle beg-gar man a beg-gin' I have been for
three score and more in this lit-tle Isle of green, And up to the Lif-fey
down to Tessague and I'm known by the name of the bold Johnnie Dhu Of
all the trades that's goin' a beg-gin' is the best. For when a man is tired he can
sit down have a rest. He begs for his din-ner, he has noth-in' else to
do, on-ly cut a-round the cor-ner with his old ri-ga doo.

I slept last night in a barn at Currabawn,
A wet night came on and I skipped through the door,
Holes in me shoes and the toes peepin' through,
Singin' skiddy-me-re-me-doodlum, for ould Johnnie Dhu.

I must be gettin' home for its gettin' late at night,
The fire's all raked and there isn't any light.
An' now you've heard me story of the ould rigadoo,
It's goodnight and God bless you from ould Johnnie Dhu.

Love Is Pleasing

Traditional, arranged by the Dubliners
(c) 1963 Heathside Music Ltd.

One of the all-time folk 'standards', this song, in its fullest
versions, includes a great many verses common to other songs.

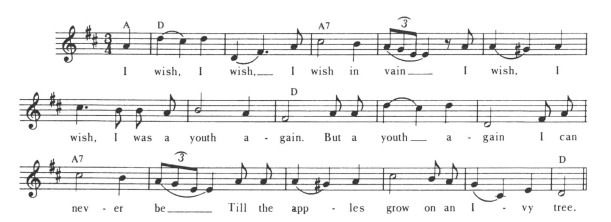

I left me father, I left me mother,
I left all me sisters and brothers too,
I left all me friends and me own relations,
I left them all for to follow you.

But the sweetest apple is the soonest rotten,
And the hottest love is the soonest cold,
And what can't be cured love has to be endured love,
And now I am bound for Americay.

Oh love is pleasing and love is teasing
And love is a pleasure when first love is new,
But as it grows older, sure love grows colder
And it fades away like the morning dew.

And love and porter makes a young man older,
And love and whisky makes him old and grey,
And what can't be cured love has to be endured love,
And now I am bound for Americay.

McAlpine's Fusiliers

Words and music by Dominic Behan
(c) Essex Music International

Dominic Behan's tribute to the boys who work on the building sites.

As down the glen came Mc - Al - pine's men with their sho-vels__ slung behind them   It was in the pub that they drank their sub or
down__ in the spike you will find them.   We sweated____ blood and we
washed down mud with quarts__ and __ pints__ of __ beer.____ But
now we're on the__ road a - gain with Mc - Al - pine's Fu - si - li - ers.

I stripped to the skin with Darky Finn down upon the Isle of Grain,
With Horseface Toole I learned the rule, no money if you stop for rain.
For McAlpine's god is a well filled hod with your
                                    shoulders cut to bits and seared,
And woe to he who looks for tea with McAlpine's Fusiliers.

I remember the day that the Bear O'Shea fell into a concrete stair,
What Horseface said, when he saw him dead, well it wasn't
                                    what the rich call prayers.
'I'm a navvy short,' was his one retort that reached unto my ears,
When the going is rough, well you must be tough with McAlpine's Fusiliers.

I've worked till the sweat near had me beat with Russian, Czech and Pole,
At shuttering jams up in the hydro dams or underneath the Thames in a hole,
I grafted hard and I got me cards and many a ganger's fist across me ears,
If you pride your life, don't join, by Christ, with McAlpine's Fusiliers.

Mrs. McGrath

Traditional, arranged by the Dubliners   (c) 1964 Heathside Music Ltd.
Between 1913-1916, this was a popular marching song of the Irish
volunteers. By a strange whimsey it is now more properly regarded
as an anti-war song.

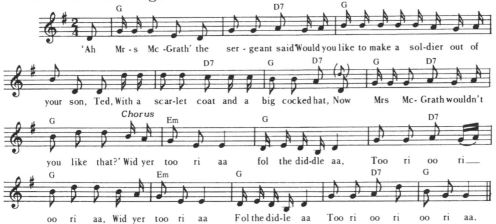

Now Mrs. McGrath lived on the sea-shore,
For the space of seven long years or more,
Till she saw a big ship sailing into the bay -
'Here's my son Ted, will ye clear the way?'

'Oh, Captain dear, where have you been?
Have you been in the Mediterreen?
Will ye tell me the news of my son Ted?
Is the poor boy living or is he dead?'

Ah well up comes Ted without any legs
And in their place he had two wooden pegs
Well she kissed him a dozen times or two
Saying, 'Glory be to God, shure it wouldn't be you!'

'Oh then were ye drunk or were ye blind
That ye left yer two fine legs behind?
Or was it while walking on the sea,
A big fish ate yer legs from the knees away?'

'Well I wasn't drunk and I wasn't blind,
When I left my two fine legs behind,
But a cannon ball on the fifth of May
Tore my two fine legs from the knees away.'

'Oh Teddy me boy,' the ould widow cried,
'Yer two fine legs were yer mammy's pride.
Them stumps of a tree wouldn't do at all -
Why didn't ye run from the big cannon ball?'

'Well all foreign wars I do proclaim
Between Don John and the King of Spain
And by herrins I'll make them rue the time
That they swept the legs from a child of mine.'

Master McGrath

Traditional, arranged by the Dubliners

Possibly, says Ronnie, the only victory the Irish ever won on English soil.

Eight-een six-ty nine being the date and the year, Those
Wa-ter-loo sportsmen and more did ap-pear For to gain the great pri-zes and
bear them a-wa', Nev-er counting on Ire-land and Mas-ter Mc-Grath.

On the twelfth of November, that day of renown,
McGrath and his keeper they left Lurgan town.
A gale in the Channel, it soon drove them o'er,
On the thirteenth they landed on England's fair shore.

Oh well when they arrived there in big London Town,
Those great English sportsmen they all gathered round,
And one of those gentlemen standing nearby
Said, 'Is that the great dog you call Master McGrath?'

Oh well one of those gentlemen standing around
Says: 'I don't care a damn for your Irish greyhound'
And another he sneered with a scornful 'Ha! Ha!
We'll soon humble the pride of your Master McGrath.'

Then Lord Lurgan came forward and said: 'Gentlemen,
If there's any amongst you has money to spend,
For your grand English nobles I don't care a straw -
Here's five thousand to one upon Master McGrath.'

Oh McGrath he looked up and he wagged his old tail.
Informing his lordship, 'Sure I know what you mane,
Don't fear, noble Brownlow, don't fear them agra,
We'll soon tarnish their laurels,' says Master McGrath.

Oh well Rose stood uncovered, the great English pride,
Her master and keeper were close by her side;
They let them away and the crowd cried: 'Hurrah'
For the pride of all England — and Master McGrath.

Oh well Rose and the Master they both ran along.
'I wonder,' says Rose, 'what took you from your home.
You should have stayed there in your Irish domain,
And not come to gain laurels on Albion's plain.'

'Well, I know,' says the Master, 'we have wild heather bogs
But, bedad, in old Ireland there's good men and dogs.
Lead on, bold Britannia, give none of your jaw,
Stuff that up your nostrils,' says Master McGrath.

Well the hare she led on just as swift as the wind
He was sometimes before her and sometimes behind,
He jumped on her back and held up his ould paw ——
'Long live the Republic,' says Master McGrath.

Nelson's Farewell

Words by Joe Dolan
Tune traditional
(c) 1966 Heathside Music Ltd.

When the Irish celebrated the fiftieth anniversary of Easter
Week by blowing Nelson off his column in Dublin's O'Connell Street,
they left the street to the effigy of the man for whom it was
named, and few tears were shed.

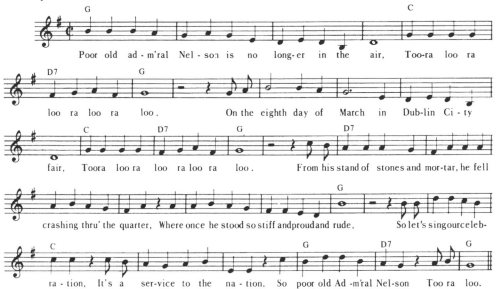

Poor old ad-m'ral Nel-son is no long-er in the air, Too-ra loo ra loo ra loo ra loo. On the eighth day of March in Dub-lin Ci-ty fair, Toora loo ra loo ra loo ra loo. From his stand of stones and mor-tar, he fell crashing thru' the quarter, Where once he stood so stiff and proud and rude, So let's sing our celeb-ra-tion, It's a ser-vice to the na-tion, So poor old Ad-m'ral Nel-son Too ra loo.

Oh fifty pounds of gelignite it sped him on his way,
  Toora loora loora looraloo,
And the lad that laid the charge, we're in debt to him today
  Toora loora loora looraloo.
In Trafalgar Square it might be fair to leave ould Nelson standing there
  But no-one tells the Irish what they'll view.
Now the Dublin Corporation can stop deliberations,
  For the boys of Ireland showed them what to do.

For a hundred and fifty seven years it stood up there in state,
  Toora loora loora looraloo,
To mark old Nelson's victory o'er the French and Spanish fleet,
  Toora loora loora looraloo.
But one-thirty in the morning, without a bit of warning,
  Old Nelson took a powder and he blew.
Oh at last the Irish nation has Parnell in higher station
  Than poor old Nelson tooraloo.

Oh the Russians and the Yanks with lunar probes they play
  Toora loora loora looraloo,
And I hear the French are trying hard to make up lost headway
  Toora loora loora looraloo.
But now the Irish join the race we have an astronaut in space
  Ireland, boys is now a world power too
So let's sing our celebration, it's a service to the nation,
  So poor old Admiral Nelson tooraloo.

The Nightingale

Traditional, arranged by the Dubliners
(c)1963 Heathside Music Ltd.

Another song that's been popular on the folk scene ever since the
first club opened.   Found in several versions with various tunes.

Out of his knapsack he took a fine fiddle,
He played her such merry tunes that you ever did hear,
He played her such merry tunes that the valley did ring,
And softly cried the fair maid as the nightingale sings.

Oh, I'm off to India for seven long years
Drinking wines and strong whiskies instead of strong beer
And if ever I return again 'twill be in the spring
And we'll both sit down together love to hear the nightingale sing.

'Well then,' says the fair maid, 'will you marry me?'
'Oh no,' says the soldier, 'however can that be?'
For I've my own wife at home in my own country
And she is the finest little maid that you ever did see.'

Off to Dublin In The Green

Traditional, arranged by the Dubliners
(c) 1966 Heathside Music Ltd.

I am a mer-ry ploughboy and I plough the fields all day till a sud-den thought came to me head, That I should roam a-way For I'm sick and tired of sla-ver-y since the day that I was born And I'm off to join the I. R. A. And I'm off to-mor-row morn.

Chorus And we're all off to Dub-lin in the green, in the green where the hel-mets glis-ten in the sun where the bay'nets flash and the rif-les crash to the rat-tle of a Thomp-son gun. *Fine*

I'll leave aside me pick and spade, I'll leave aside me plough
I'll leave aside me horse and yoke, I no longer need them now.
I'll leave aside me Mary, she's the girl that I adore,
And I wonder if she'll think of me when she hears the rifles roar.

And when the war is over, and dear old Ireland is free,
I'll take her to the church to wed and a rebel's wife she'll be.
Well some men fight for silver and some men fight for gold,
But the I.R.A. are fighting for the land that the Saxons stole.

The Ould Orange Flute

Traditional, arranged by the Dubliners
(c) 1964 Heathside Music Ltd.

As one noted Catholic politician said when he sang this ballad,
'It's a fine song - 'tis a pity it's on the wrong side!'

But Bob, the deceiver, he took us all in,
He married a Papish called Bridget McGinn,
Turned Papish himself and forsook the old cause
That gave us our freedom, religion and laws.
Now the boys in the place made some comment upon it,
And Bob had to fly to the province of Connacht,
Well he fled with his wife and his fixings to boot,
And along with the latter his ould Orange flute.

At the chapel on Sundays, to atone for past deeds,
He'd say Paters and Aves, and he counted his beads,
Till, after some time, at the priest's own desire,
Bob went with his ould flute to play in the choir.
Well he went with his ould flute to play in the mass,
But the instrument shivered and sighed, oh alas,
And, blow as he would, though it made a great noise,
The flute would play only 'The protestant boys.'

At a council of priests that was held the next day,
They decided to banish the ould flute away.
They couldn't knock heresy out of its head,
So they bought Bob a new one to play in its stead.
Now the ould flute it was doomed and its fate was pathetic;
'Twas fastened and burnt at the stake as heretic.
As the flames roared around it, sure they heard a strange noise -
'Twas the ould flute still playing 'The protestant boys.'

The Patriot Game

Words and music by Dominic Behan
(c) 1962 Clifford Music Ltd.

This song, about the death of Fergal O'Hanlon, who tried to
abolish the border between the Six Counties and the Republic,
has become world famous. Undoubtedly one of the best ballads
ever to come out of the Irish struggles.

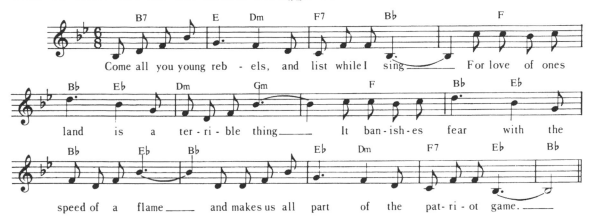

My name is O'Hanlon, I'm just gone sixteen,
My home is in Monoghan there I was weaned,
I learned all my life cruel England to blame
And so I'm a part of the patriot game.

It's barely a year since I wandered away
With the local battalions of the bold I.R.A.
I read of our heroes and wanted the same
To play up my part in the patriot game.

They told me how Connolly was shot in a chair
His wounds from the fighting all bleeding and bare,
His fine body twisted all battered and lame,
They soon made me part of the patriot game.

This Ireland of mine has for long been half-free,
Six Counties are under John Bull's Monarchy,
But still DeValera is greatly to blame,
For shirking his part in the patriot game.

I don't mind a bit if I shoot down police,
They are lackeys for war never guardians of peace,
And yet at deserters I'm never let aim,
The rebels who sold out the patriot game.

And now as I lie with my body all holes,
I think of those traitors who bargained and sold.
I'm sorry my rifle has not done the same
For the Quislings who sold out the patriot game.

The Ould Woman From Wexford

Traditional, arranged by the Dubliners
(c) 1964 Heathside Music Ltd.

Known also as <u>Marrow Bones</u> and <u>The Blind Man He Could See</u>,
this song exists in several versions, all of which tell how the
man outwitted his treacherous wife.

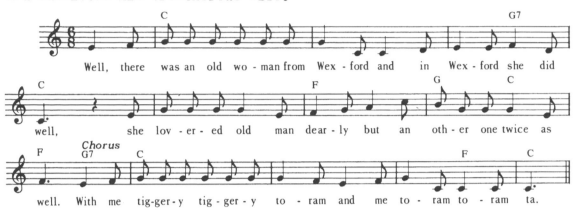

Well, there was an old wo-man from Wex-ford and in Wex-ford she did
well, she lov-er-ed old man dear-ly but an oth-er one twice as
well. *Chorus* With me tig-ger-y tig-ger-y to-ram and me to-ram to-ram ta.

Ah one day she went to a doctor
Some medicine for to find.
She said, 'Will ye give me something
That'll make me ould man blind?'

Says he, 'Give him eggs and marrow bones
And make him sup them all,
And it won't be so very long after
That he won't see you at all.'

Well the doctor wrote a letter
And he signed it with his hand.
He sent it to the ould man
Just to let him understand.

So she fed him the eggs and the marrow bones;
And she made him sup them all,
And it wasn't so very long after
That he couldn't see the wall.

Says th'ould man 'I think I'll drown meself,
But that might be a sin.'
Says she, 'I'll come along with you
And I'll help to shove you in.'

Well the ould woman she stood back a bit
For to rush an' push him in,
But the ould man gently stepped aside,
And she went tumblin' in.

Oh, how loudly she did yell
And how loudly she did bawl
'Arra, hould yer whist, y'ould woman,
Sure I can't see you at all.

Ah, sure eggs, eggs and marrow bones
Will make yer ould man blind,
But, if you want to drown him,
You must creep up close behind
    With me tiggery, tiggery-toram,
    And me toram-toram-ta,
    With me tiggery, tiggery-toram,
    And the blind man he could see.

The Peatbog Soldiers

Reputed to have been written by an inmate of one of Hitler's
prison camps, this fine song has been translated from the German
and sung in many languages.

Up and down the guards are pacing,
No one, no one can go through.
Flight would mean a sure death facing;
Guns and barbed wire greet our view.

But for us there's no complaining,
Winter will in time be past;
One day we shall cry rejoicing,
'Homeland dear, you're mine at last!'

(Final chorus)

Then will the peat-bog soldiers
March no more with their spades
To the moor.

Wohin auch das Auge blicket
Moor und Heide ringsherum.
Vogelsang uns nicht erquicket,
Eichen stehen kahl und krumm.
   Wir sind die Moorsoldaten
   Und ziehen mit dem Spaten,
   Ins Moor.

Auf und nieder gehen die Posten,
Keiner, keiner kann hindurch.
Flucht wird nur das Leben kosten
Fielfach ist umzäunt die Burg.
   Wir sind die Moorsoldaten
   Und ziehen mit dem Spaten,
   Ins Moor.

Doch Für uns gibt es kein Klagen,
Ewig kann's nicht Winter sein.
Einmal werden froh wir sagen,
'Heimat, du bist wieder mein.'
   Dann ziehen die Moorsoldaten
   NICHT mehr mit dem Spaten
   Ins Moor.

Preab San Ol

Traditional, arranged by the Dubliners
(c) 1963 Heathside Music Ltd.

The title means 'jump into drinking' - or 'what's your gargle?'
- or 'another round'. Translated from the Gaelic.

Why spend your lei - sure be -reft of plea-sure a -mas-sing trea -sure why scrape and save? Why look so can -ny at ev -'ry pen - ny? You'll take no mon - ey with-in the grave Landlords and gen - try with all their plen - ty must still go emp - ty where 'er they're bound. So to my think-ing we'd best be drink-ing our glasses clink-ing and round and round.

King Solomon's glory, so famed in story,
Was far outshone by the lilies guise,
But hard winds harden both field and garden,
Pleading for pardon, the lily dies.
Life's but a bauble of toil and trouble,
The feathered arrow, once shot ne'er found,
So, lads and lasses, because life passes,
Come fill your glasses for another round.

The huckster greedy, he blinds the needy.
Their strifes unheeding, shouts 'Money down!'
His special vices, his fancy prices,
For a florin value he'll charge a crown.
With hump for tramel, the scripture's camel
Missed the needle's eye and so came to ground.
Why pine for riches, while still you've stitches
To hold your britches up? Another round!

The Rare Ould Mountain Dew

Traditional, arranged by the Dubliners
(c) 1964 Heathside Music Ltd.

Let grasses grow and waters flow In a free and ea-sy way, But give me e-nough of the rare old stuff that's made near Gal-way Bay, Come gan-gers all from Don-e-gal, Sli-go and Lei-trim too, Oh, we'll give them the slip and we'll take a sip of the rare old Moun-tain Dew. Hi the dith-er-y al the dal, dal the dal the dithery al, al the dal, dal dith-er-y al dee Hi the dith-er-y al the dal, dal the dal the dith-er-y al dal the dal dal dith-er-y al the dee.___

There's a neat little still at the foot of the hill,
Where the smoke curls up to the sky;
By a whiff of the smell you can plainly tell
That there's poitín, boys, close by.
For it fills the air with a perfume rare,
And betwixt both me and you,
As home we roll, we can drink a bowl,
Or a bucketful of mountain dew.

Now learned men as use the pen,
Have writ the praises high
Of the rare poitín from Ireland green,
Distilled from wheat and rye.
Away with yer pills, it'll cure all ills,
Be ye Pagan, Christian or Jew;
So take off your coat and grease your throat
With a bucketful of mountain dew.

Ratcliffe Highway

Traditional, arranged by the Dubliners
(c) 1963 Heathside Music Ltd.

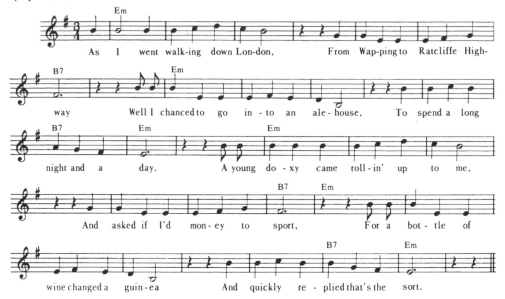

A young doxy came rollin' up to me,
And asked if I'd money to sport,
For a bottle of wine changed a guinea
And quickly replied, 'That's the sort!'

When the bottle was put on the table,
There were glasses for everyone.
When I asked for the change of me guinea,
She tipped me the verse of a song.

This lady flew into a passion,
She placed both her hands on her hips,
Sayin', 'Sailor, don't you know now our fashion,
Do you think you're on board of your ship?'

'Well if this is your fashion to rob me,
It's a fashion that I won't abide,
So launch out the change of me guinea,
Or I'll give to you a broadside.'

A gold watch hung over the mantel,
So the change of me guinea I take,
And down the stairs I run nimbly,
Sayin', 'Damn me old boots I'm well paid.'

Well the night it being dark in me favour,
To the river I quickly did creep,
I got into a boat bound for Deptford,
Got safely on board of me ship.

So come all of you young sailors,
That ramble down Ratcliffe Highway,
If you chance to go into an alehouse,
Be careful how long, lad, you stay.

For the wines and the women invite you,
And your heart will be all in a rage,
If you give them a guinea for a bottle,
You can go to the devil for your change.

The Rocky Road to Dublin

Traditional, arranged by the Dubliners
(c) 1963 Heathside Music Ltd.

A bit of a terror to sing, this became one of the Dubliners'
showpieces.   The tune is a favourite with fiddlers and pipers.

While in the mer-ry month of May from my home I start-ed,
left the girls of Tu-am near-ly brok-en heart-ed, sa-lut-ed fath-er dear, kissed me
dar-lin' moth-er, drank a pint of beer me grief and fears to smoth-er, Then
off to reap the corn, and leave where I was born, cut a stout blackthorn to ban-ish
ghost and gob-lin In a brand new pair of brogues I ratt-led o'er the the bogs and
fright-ened all the dogs on the rock-y road to Dub-i-lin. One, two,
three, four, five hunt the hare and turn her down the
rock-y road and all the ways to Dub-i-lin, whack fol-al-de-rol.

In Mullingar that night I rested limbs so weary
Started by daylight next morning light and airy,
Took a drop o' the pure, to keep me heart from sinkin',
That's the Paddy's cure whenever he's on for drinkin'.
To see the lassies smile, laughin' all the while,
At me curious style, 'twould set your heart a-bubblin',
They ax'd if I was hired, the wages I required,
Till I was almost tired of the rocky road to Dublin.

In Dublin next arrived, I thought it such a pity
To be so soon deprived a view of that fine city,
Then I took a stroll, all among the quality
Me bundle it was stole in a neat locality;
Something crossed me mind, then I looked behind,
No bundle could I find upon me stick a-wobblin',
Enquirin' after the rogue, they said me Connacht brogue
Wasn't much in vogue, on the rocky road to Dublin.

From there I got away, me spirits never failin',
Landed on the quay just as the ship was sailin',
Captain at me roared, said that no room had he,
When I jumped aboard, a cabin found for Paddy
Down among the pigs, I skipped some funny rigs,
I played some hearty jigs, the water round me bubblin',
When off Holyhead, I wished meself was dead,
Or, better far instead, on the rocky road to Dublin.

The boys of Liverpool, when we safely landed
Called myself a fool, I could no longer stand it;
Blood began to boil, temper I was losin'
Poor ould Erin's isle they began abusin',
'Hurrah me soul,' says I, my shillelagh I let fly,
Some Galway boys were by, saw I was a hobblin',
Then with loud hurray, they joined in the affray,
We quickly cleared the way for the rocky road to Dublin.

Roddy McCorley

Traditional, arranged by the Dubliners
(c) 1969 Heathside Music Ltd.

Another ballad of the 1798 rising.

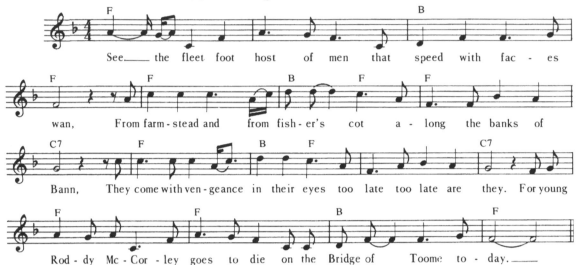

See___ the fleet foot host of men that speed with fac - es
wan, From farm-stead and from fish-er's cot a - long the banks of
Bann, They come with ven-geance in their eyes too late too late are they. For young
Rod - dy Mc - Cor - ley goes to die on the Bridge of Toome to - day.___

Up the narrow street he steps
Smiling, proud and young.
About the hemp rope on his neck
The golden ringlets clung
There was never a tear in his blue eye,
Both sad and bright are they,
For young Roddy McCorley goes to die
On the bridge of Toome today.

When he last stepped up that street,
His shining pike in hand,
Behind him marched in grim array
A stalwart, earnest band.
For Antrim town, for Antrim town,
He led them to the fray,
And young Roddy McCorley goes to die
On the bridge of Toome today.

There was never a one of all your dead
More bravely fell in fray
Than he who marches to his fate
On the bridge of Toome today.
True to the last, true to the last,
He treads the upward way,
And young Roddy McCorley goes to die
On the bridge of Toome today.

Surrounded By Water

Words by Dominic Behan.   Tune traditional.
(c) Essex Music International.

Dominic Behan's tribute to <u>The Sea Around Us</u> (by which title it is
also known). That last line sometimes gets rendered 'Thank God
<u>it's</u> surrounded by water', as a tribute to the strength of Irish
whiskey.

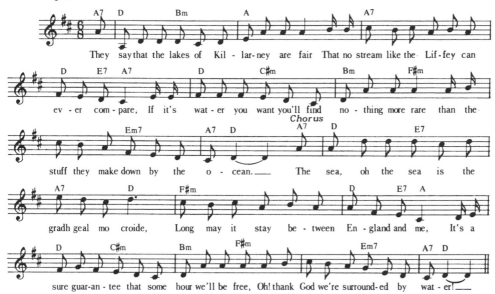

Tom Moore made his waters meet fame and renown,
A great lover of anything dressed in a crown;
In brandy the bandy old Saxon he'd drown,
But throw ne'er a one into the ocean.

The Scots have their whisky, the Welsh have their speech,
And their poets are paid about tenpence a week,
Provided no hard words on England they speak;
Oh Lord! What a price for devotion!

The Danes came to Ireland with nothing to do
But dream of the plundered old Irish they slew;
'Yeh will in your Vikings,' said Brian Boru,
And threw them back in the ocean!

Two foreign old monarchs in battle did join,
Each wanting their head on the back of a coin:
If the Irish had sense they'd drown both in the Boyne
And Partition throw into the ocean!

Three Lovely Lassies from Kimmage

Traditional, arranged by the Dubliners
(c) 1963 Heathside Music Ltd.

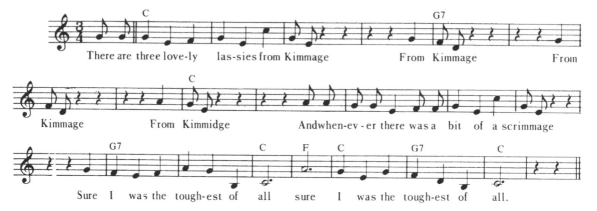

Well the cause of the row is Joe Cashin,
Joe Cashin, Joe Cashin, Joe Cashin,
For he told me he thought I looked smashin'
At a dance at the Adelaide Hall,
At a dance at the Adelaide Hall.

He told me he thought we should marry,
Should marry, should marry, should marry,
He said it was foolish to tarry,
So he lent me the price of a ring,
So he lent me the price of a ring.

When he gets a few jars he goes frantic,
Goes frantic, goes frantic, goes frantic,
Well he's tall and he's dark and romantic,
And I love him in spite of it all,
And I love him in spite of it all.

Well me dad said he'd give us a present,
A present, a present, a present,
A stool and a lovely stuffed pheasant,
And a picture to hang on the wall,
And a picture to hang on the wall.

I went down to the tenancy section,
The section, the section, the section,
The T.D. just before the election,
Said he'd get me a house near me ma,
Said he'd get me a house near me ma.

Well I'm getting a house the man said it,
Man said it, man said it, man said it,
When I've five or six kids to me credit,
In the meantime we'll live with me ma,
In the meantime we'll live with me ma.

The Twang Man

Traditional, arranged by the Dubliners
(c) 1964 Heathside Music Ltd.

A rare bit of old Dublin from a broadsheet ballad.   The tune is
Limerick Is Beautiful.

Come, list-en to me sto-ry, 'Tis a-bout a nice young man, When the Mil-
ee-tia was-n't want-in' He dealt in hawk-ing twang. He
loved a love-ly mai-den As fair as a-ny midge, An' she
kep' a tray-cle de-pot Wan side of the Car-lisle Bridge.

Another wan came a coortin' her,
His name was Mickey Bags,
He was a commercial traveller,
An' he dealt in bones and rags.
Well he took her out to **Sandymount**
For to see the waters rowl,
An' he stole the heart of the Twangman's girl
Playin' Billy-in-the-Bowl!

Oh when the twangman heard of that
He flew into a terrible rage,
An' he swore be the contents of his twang cart
On him he'd have revenge.
So he stood in wait near James's gate,
Till the poor old Bags came up,
With his twang knife, sure he tuk the lief
Of the poor ould gather' em-up!

Take Me Up to Monto

Monto - Montgomery Street - was in a 'red-light' district of
Dublin, bounded by Gardiner Street, Sherriff Street, and the Gloster
Diamond.
<u>Liathroidi</u> = balls
<u>Pog mo thoin</u> = kiss my arse

Well if you've got a win-go, take her up to Rin-go, Where the wax-ies sing o
all the day, If you've had your fill of por-ter and you can't go a-ny fur-ther, Just
give your men the or-der, 'Back to the Quay'. And take her up to Mon-to, Mon-to,
Mon-to, Take her up to Mon-to lan-ger-oo. ! ! to you!__

You've heard of Butcher Foster, the dirty old imposter,
He took a mot and lost her up the Furry Glen.
He first put on his bowler, then he buttoned up his trousers,
And he whistled for a growler and he said 'My men,
    Take me up to Monto, Monto, Monto.......

The fairy told him, 'Skin the goat'; O'Donnell put him on the boat,
He wished he'd never been afloat, the dirty skite.
It wasn't very sensible to tell on the Invincibles
They took aboard the principals, day and night
    Be goin' up to Monto, Monto, Monto.......

You've seen the Dublin Fusiliers, the dirty old bamboozaliers,
They went and got the childer, one, two, three.
Marchin' from the Linen Hall, there's one for every cannon ball
And Vicky's goin' to send youse all o'er the sea.
    But first go up to Monto, Monto, Monto......

When the Czar of Rooshia, and the King of Prooshia
Landed in the Phoenix in a big balloon,
They asked the Garda band to play The Wearin' o' the Green
But the buggers in the depot didn't know the tune,
    So they both went up to Monto, Monto, Monto......

The Queen she came to call on us, she wanted to see all of us,
I'm glad she didn't fall on us, she's eighteen stone.
'Mr. Neill, Lord Mayor,' says she, 'Is this all you've got to show to me?'
'Why no, ma'am, there's some more to see - póg mo thóin
    And he took her up to Monto, Monto, Monto,
    Took her up to Monto, langer oo.
    Líathróidí to you.

Walking In The Dew

Traditional, arranged by the Dubliners
(c) 1963 Heathside Music Ltd.

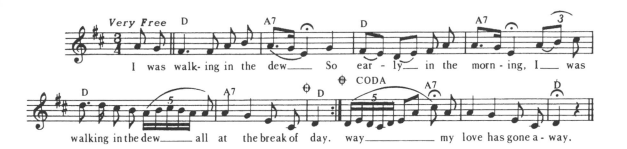

Very Free

I was walk-ing in the dew___ So ear - ly___ in the morn - ing, I___ was

walking in the dew___ all at the break of day. way_____ my love has gone a - way.

I was strolling with my love, so early in the morning,
I was strolling with my love, all at the break of day.

Oh and now the sun is setting, and I am walking all alone,
I am walking all alone, 'cause my love has gone away,
My love has gone away.

The Wild Rover

Traditional, arranged by the Dubliners
(c) 1963 Heathside Music Ltd.

Almost the Irishman's trademark on the folk scene.

I've been a wild rov-er for ma-ny's the year,___ And I've spent all me money on whis-key and beer But now I'm re-turn-ing with gold in great store And I nev-er will play the wild rov-er no more, and it's No, Nay, nev-er,___ no, nay nev-er no more__ will I play__ the wild rov-er,___ no never___ no more.__

I brought up from me pocket ten sovereigns bright,
And the landlady's eyes opened wide with delight.
She said, 'I have whiskeys and wines of the best
And the words that you told me were only in jest'

I'll go home to my parents, confess what I've done,
And I'll ask them to pardon their prodigal son.
And, when they've caressed me as oft times before,
I never will play the wild rover no more.

Will Ye Come To The Bower?

Traditional, arranged by the Dubliners
(c) 1966 Heathside Music Ltd.

Will you come to the bower o'er the free bound-less o - cean where stu-pend-u-ous waves roll in thun-der and mo-tion where the fair maids are seen and the wild tem-pest gath-ers,to loved Er - in the green the dear land of our fath-ers? Will you come, will you, will you, will you come to the bow-er?

Will you come to the land of O'Neill and O'Donnell,
Of Lord Lucan of old and the immortal O'Connell
Where Brian chased the Dane and St.Patrick the vermin,
And whose valleys remain still most beautiful and charming?

You can visit Benburb and the stormy Blackwater,
Where Owen Roe met Munroe and his chieftains did slaughter,
Where the lambs sport and play on the mossy all over,
From those bright golden views to enchanting Restrevor.

You can see Dublin city and the fine groves of Blarney,
The Baun, Boyne, and Liffey, and the lakes of Killarney,
You can ride on the tide o'er the broad majestic Shannon,
You can sail round Loch Neagh and see storied Dungannon.

You can visit New Ross, gallant Wexford and Gorey,
Where the green was last seen by proud Saxon and Tory,
Where the soil is sanctified by the blood of each true man,
Where they died satisfied their enemies they would not run from.

Will you come and awake our dear land from its slumber,
And her fetters we will break links that long are encumbered,
And the air will resound with hosannas to greet you,
On the shore will be found gallant Irishmen to meet you.

Willie Gannon

Traditional, arranged by the Dubliners
(c) 1964 Heathside Music Ltd.

Obviously of recent vintage and sung beautifully by Ronnie on a
now-deleted ep record.

Come all you young fell-ows and lis-ten to my song, It's all about a
young man and he did a great wrong. His name was Wil-lie Gannon and he lived down in
Bray, Well he killed a po - lice - man and the law made him pay.

The law watched young Gannon, each turn that he made,
When he broke one bylaw with a belt of his spade.
He struck the death blow when he turned his broad back,
And he left him there lying where the Dargle runs black.

Willie Gannon was convicted and sentenced to die,
Now his enemies could't laugh but his friends couldn't cry.
When he brought down the uniform on that bright summer day,
Farewell Willie Gannon, now you sleep 'neath the clay.